THE EXAMINATION AND TRYAL OF OLD FATHER CHRISTMAS

JOSIAH KING

FV Editions

Behold the maiestie and grace
of loueing, cheerfull, Christmas face,
Whome many thousands with one breath:
Cry, out let him be put to death.
Who indeede can neuer die:
So long as man hath memory.

THE EXAMINATION AND
Tryal of OLD Father *CHRISTMAS*
Together with his Clearing by
the JURY,
At the Assizes held at the Town
of *Difference*, in the County
Of *Discontent*.
Written according to Legal Proceeding,
by *Josiah King.*
LONDON,
Printed for *Charles Brome*, at the *Gun*
at the West End of S. *Pauls.* 1686

CONTENTS

To the Worshipful John Hodge, Doctor of Physick at Modbury in Devon.

Sir:

Pardon I beseech you my presumption, in presenting you this insuing Allegory: I must confess, it is too trivial for your grave perusal, yet the reading perhaps may serve to the same end the writing did, which was only Recreation; Fancy is a Daughter of *Salomons* good Houswife; she will bee spinning before it bee light: Sir, I hope you will *Candidly* construe his intention, who is weak in his inIdeavours, though strong in his desires, and if he could he would not; or if he would, he could not, be otherwise than

> Your Servant in the bonds
> of affection.
> Josiah King.

To Captain *Thomas Prinne,* of *Wembury.*

Sir,

In *discharge of my promise, I here tender you the*

service of an old man, let him not be served,
like the Serving-man, turned away because old;
I hope he will not speak any thing that may of-
fend a chaste ear; yes I question not, but there
will be evil reports raised on him, and indeed,
Woe were to him, if all should speak well of him.

> *I know you are ingenious, and besides*
> *I have been told, a lover of good Tydes;*
> *O let them flow, if they content do*
> > *bring;*
> *But never ebb; thus praise your Servant*
> King.

To **Momus** *or the* **Critick.**

Self-conceited Sir,

I Know thou wilt brag, thy very breath is enough to poison the Muses; how many pots of oyntment hast thou spoiled? I know thou wilt be choping upon my broken stile; But tell me, canst thou expect flowers from him, that never walkt in *Apollo's* Garden? If thou sayest, here is something stoln, I say, thou leyst; it is but borrowed and that is the Method. The Author of the Isle of Man, and I, had it from the Assizes; now be advised by me, put thy ears in under thy cap, and shut thy black

mouth, and then no body will know thee; Thus
faith

J. K.

To the honest Reader.

Friend,

My *intent in writing this Alegorical Tryal of*
Christmas, *was not to vent mine opinion upon the ob-*
servation of the time, be that observes a day as he
should, may keep Christmas every day; only herein is
expressed some part of those Arguments which are used
in pleading for, or against the keeping of it. It will be, I
hope, no cause of controversie, there is too much divi-
sion already, for which there is as much grief of heart:
Pray *for the peace of* Jerusalem, *let them prosper*
that love it.

> *Blessed are those that all dissention hate,*
> *And strive to quiet a disturbed state.*

Vale.

THE TRYALL OF CHRISTMAS.

The day appointed for the Assizes being come, the Judge and the Sheriff, with the Justices of the Peace, came to the place where they were to sit: and first I think it would not be amiss to tell you the Names of them; the Judge was called, Judge *Hate-bate*, the Sheriffs name was called *Leonard Love-peace*; the Justices are called as followeth; the first is Justice *Hate-bribe,,* the second is Justice *Wife*, the third Justice *Upright*, the fourth Justice *Do-good,,* the fifth Justice *Fear-none;* these with the Judge and Sheriff, being settled on the Bench, the Judge read his Commission, after which, the chief of the Prisoners, being one old *Christmas*, was commanded to be brought to the Bar, when was a Jury for Life and Death to be im-panneld, who are for the Common-wealth, and are to give in their Vertict according to their Evidence, and as they were to be called, there stept up one Sir *Hica Busy*, and delivered a list to the Sheriff, informing him that the Country desired those men, whose names were set down, might be the Jury to pass upon old *Christmas* at the Bar; which the Sheriff for quietness sake, delivered to the Clerk of the Arraignment, to have them called, a company of brave Gentlemen, you shall hear them named by and by.

The Clerk having received the Paper, bid the Cryer call, as followeth

Cler. Cryer, call Mr. *Starve-mouse.*

Cr. O yes, Mr. *Starve-mouse.*

Cryer, call Mr. *All-pride.*

Cr. O yes, Mr. *All-pride.*

Cryer, call Mr. *Keep-all.*

Cr. O yes, Mr. *Keep-all.*

Cryer, call Mr. *Love-none.*

Cr. O yes, Mr. *Love-none.*

Cryer, call Mr. *Eat-alone.*

Cr. O yes, Mr. *Eat-alone.*

Cryer, call Mr. *Give-little.*

Cr. O yes, Mr. *Give-little.*

Cryer, call Mr. *Hoord Corn.*

Cr. O yes, Mr *Hoord Corn.*

Cryer, call Mr. *Gruntch-meat.*

Cr. O yes, Mr. *Gruntch-meat.*

Cryer, call Mr. *Knit-gut.*

Cr. O yes, Mr. *Knit-gut.*

Cryer, call Mr. *Serve-time.*

Cr. O yes, Mr. *Serve-time.*

Cryer, call Mr. *Hate-good.*

Cr. O yes, Mr. *Hate-good.*

Cryer, call Mr. *Cold-kitchin.*

Cr. O yes, Mr. *Cold-kitchen.*

Then saith the *Clerk* to the *Cryer,* count them, *Starve-mouse* one, *All-pride* two, *Keep-all* three, *Love-none* four, *Eat-alone* five, *Give-little* six, *Hoord-corn* seven, *Gruntch-meat* eight, *Knit-gut* nine, *Serve-time* ten, *Hate-good* eleven, *Cold-kitchin* twelve.

Then saith the *Cryer,* all you bountiful Gentlemen of the Jury, answer to your names, and stand together and hear your Charge.

With that there was such a lamentable groan heard, enough to turn Ice into Ashes, which caused the *Judge,* and the rest of the Bench, to demand what the matter was; it was replied, that the grave old Gentleman *Christmas,* did sound at the nameing of the Jury; then it was commanded that they should give him air, and comfort him up, so that he might plead for himself: and here I cannot pass by in silence the love that was expressed by the Country people, some shreeking and crying for the old man; others striving to hold him up.

Others hugging him, till they had almost broke the back of him, others running for Cordials, and strong-waters, insomuch as [?] last they had called back his wandring spirits which were ready to take their last farewell.

Then said the *Judge*, old man, what is the matter?

Christm. Ah good my Lord! I have been grosly abused, & had been troden under foot had not these good Country people helpt me.

Judg. But methought I hears some say, it was at the nameing of the Jury; If thou hast ought justly to except against them, I will hear thee.

Christm. I heartily thank your Honour, and this favour which your Lordship hath granted me, hath encouraged me to crave another, and that is, That you be pleased to grant me the benefit of a Council, in regard of mine Age, and defect of memory and expression. Besides, the Jury are all strangers to me, as well as enemies; and therefore I desire my Council may be one of this County, that so he may describe the Gentlemen of the Jury.

Judg. Well *Christmas*, in regard that thou wert a merry old man when I was but a boy, & did often at thy coming make me sport, I have granted thy request, chuse thy Councillor,

Christm. I humbly thank your goodness, my Lord.

Then the old man whispered to a friend, to deliver a Fee to Councillor *Erab*, and desire him to decypher the Jury, and as occasion did offer it self, to plead his Cause.

The Fee being delivered, and accepted, the Councillor after this manner spake to the Bench.

Council. My Lord, may it please your Honour, this Jury which is now impanneld, and to pass their Verdict upon Old *Christmas*, is illegally chosen, there is not one of them a Free-man, and all mortal enemies to this old Gentleman.

And first of all here is Mr. *Starve-mouse*, I wonder how he dare shew face in Court, the very Cats cannot abide him.

Secondly, Here is Mr. *All-pride*, I must confess he hath an estate.

> But at his house-keeping you may
>   admire,
> Where silken gowns do quench
>   thekitchin fire;
> And of his Cup, there's noe that ever
>   taste,
> And break their necks may sooner
>   than their fast.

> And when at any time a Feast bee'l
>   keep,

He is Bravado will kill half a Sheep.

Here's another, my Lord, call'd *Eat-alone*, a Malefactor my Lord, & ought to be condemned by *Magna Charta;* where it is to be found that one of the Lord chief Justices own Clerks being accused, was forced to free himself, and get it recorded, that he eat not his morsel alone. To be short my Lord,

> To eat his breakfast he a corner
> sought,
> And in his pocket hath his dinner
> brought,

There's another of them called *Give-little*, he may well be called give nothing, yet the Fool will sometimes brag of his Charity; if he kills but an Egg, and give the offall to the needy, he is, my Lord, a great Benefactor to the poor, but will bestow nothing upon the beggars; and as for Master *Cold-kitchin*, here is his man *Sam, Servant,* is ready to give Oath, that he hath almost starved him to death.

And for Mr. *Hoord-corn*, the people in general all curse him, it is he that makes the Epha small, and the Shekel great; good my Lord, let Justice be done upon him, unless he will save *Gregory* the labour, and follow the steps of his Father, who the last cheap year hanged himself,

There's onother of them call'd Mr. *Grutch-meat*, he may be termed Grutch-cloaths too, for his cloaths were never young in my memory, and they may be set down in the Almanack with the dear year, & the great frost, he is one that never gave Als in his life, the house o his own body he will not keep Tenantable, but it has been irrecoverably decayed, had it not been for the reparations of other mens Tables where he hoords up meat enough for a month; in a word, My Lord, he is a base fellow, and so I leave him.

There's another of them call'd Mr. *Serve-time*, he dwells at the sign of the Weather-cock; he hath a glove for every hand, he holds it most safe to do as most do, right or wrong, he will be on the harder side.

> And when a hunting goes, I have
>   been told
> He with the Hare will run, and
>   Hound will hold.

So my Lord, not fot for a Juror, because he makes conscience of nothing.

Judg. Were there ever such a brood of Vipers as these? Mr. *Sheriff,* how came this to pass?

Sheriff. Surely my Lord, it was Sir *Hica Busy* that gave me the List, and told me, it was the Countries desire that these men should be the Jury, and I was induced to believe it, in regard I know him to be a popular-man.

With this the Jury began to murmur, and told the Judge that the Councillor had abused them to please his Client, as most of his fraternity will do, and therefore would appear, or stand to justifiction.

Council. My Lord, here are some witnesses to prove the truth of what I have spoken.

Judg. Let them come in.

Counc. Cryer, call *Humility.*

Cr. O yes, *Humility.*

Judg. Come friend, can you testifie any thing against any of the Jury?

Hum. My Lord, I am convinced, that all that hath been spoken by the Worshipful Councillor is true, but especially I can speak something more against Mr. *All-pride,* than hath been yet declared: for may it please your Honour, he hath endeavoured to murder me, and my Neighbour *Patience:* and his practice is in brave cloaths, bigg looks, swearing and swaggering, & insulting over his poor Neighbours; there was one Mr. *Good-work* lived in the house before this fellow threw him out of the doors; he spent more in Mustard every year than his gaudy Gentleman doth in Beef; he keeps two wicked men to his Servants, the one is called *Stony-heart,* the other *Bribe,* and these help to keep him up in his wicked courses.

My Lord, here are many more witnesses, if your Lordship please to examine them.

Judg. No, no, this is not *Joshua's* day; Mr. *Sheriff,* let another Jury be impanneld immediately, a pack like the former, if they be to be gotten.

Council.

Before he find their Fellows, he
    must rake
Tophet throughout, and the infernal
    Lake.

The jury being chosen, were called, as followeth.

Mr. *Love-friend* one.

Mr. *Hate-strife* two.

Mr. *Free-man* three.

Mr. *Cloath-back* four.

Mr. *Warm-gut* five.

Mr. *Goodwork* six.

Mr. *Neighbour-hood* seven.

Mr. *Ope-house* eight.

Mr. *Scorn-use* nine.

Mr. *Soft-heart* ten.

Mr. *Merry-man* eleven.

Mr. *True-love* twelve.

No man taking any exception against this Jury, the Clerk read the Inditement against old *Christmas*, as followeth.

Cler. Christmas hearken to thy Inditement, *Christmas* thou art here indited by the name of *Christmas*, of the Town of *Superstition,* in the County of *Idolatry,* and that thou hast from time to time, abused the people of this Common-wealth, drawing and inticing them to Drunkenness, gluttony, & unlawful Gaming, Wantonness, Uncleanness, Lasciviousness, Cursing, Swearing, abuse of the Creatures, some to one Vice, and some to another; all to Idleness: what sayest thou to thy Inditement, guilty, or not guilty? He answered, not guilty, and so put himself to the Trial.

After this, the Parties that can give Evidence against him are called.

Councillor

His innocence appears, I law a
    Crown,
Whiter than untrod Snow, er Culver
    down.

Cler. Cryer, call in *Gregory Grutch-meat.*

O yes, *Gregory Grutch-meat.*

Judg. Come you Thin-belly, what can you say against the Prisoner at the Bar, dost thou know him?

Greg. Know him? Yes my Lord, his name is *Christmas*, a great waster and Spendthrift, he hath been all his days, nothing like *Sampsons* Lion, *Out of that eater came forth meat*, but this old fellow devours all, and produces nothing, he passes the grat eater of *Kent*, his mind is wholly set upon his belly, for satisfaction of which, he murders the poor innocent creatures; My Lord, let the Records be searcht, & before the flood, we cannot find, that man ever eat any thing but fruit or herbs, but this Cormorant is all for flesh, flesh, & eats it with the blood thereof, which is the cause that he is so beastly minded, a meer *Esau*, he will sell his birthright to satisfie his belly, he is a Bastard, begotten of the Horseleeches daughter, continually crying, *Give, Give;* some people of this Nation, are so besotted by this old fool, that they make a world of provision against his coming, & invite him to be Gossip to all their Pyes, and call them after his name, *Christmas-Pyes.*

My Lord, here is an honest Neighbour of mine called *Pinch-gut,* can testify as much as my self.

Council.

Here me a word my Lord, and if you
please,
Paraohs ill-favoured Kine were fed
by these.

Cler. Cryer, call *Pinch-gut.*

Cr. O yes, Mr. *Pinch-gut.*

Judg. Come fellow, what can you say against
the Prisoner?

Pinch. I perceive my Lord, the Councillor is
purposed to abuse us, to please his Client, as all
the fraternity will do: but I would have him know,
that I was well descended, My Father was called
Saving, & my Mother's name was *Spare,* a very
good housewife, and of great repute amongst the
Farmers.

Judg. Fellow, I am not come her to examine
pedigrees, were they as authentick as a
Welchmans. But come, let me hear what thou canst
say in the behalf of the Common-wealth, against
the Prisoner at the Bar.

Pinch-gut. My Lord, I can say that this Old man
is an Epicure, all his delight is to please his Palat,
his throat is an open Sepulchure, he is the canker
of the Common-wealth, worse than the Locust, or
the *Palmer* worm, and this is the sum of what I can
testifie.

Council.

This is a liberal fellow 'tis confest,
He will keep all, and give away the
    rest.

Judg. What witnesses are there more?
Clerk. Call Mr *Allwork.*
Cr. O yes, Mr. *Allwork, Allwork, Allwork.*
Judg. Friend, What's the matter you must have so much calling, and so long coming?
Counc.

It must be so my Lord, even snails
    keep state,
When with slow pace, their horns
    peep forth the gate.

Allwork. I was very busie my Lord, in my shop.

Judg. Can you evidence anything against the Prisoner?

Allw. I can witness that he is a very idle fellow: I saw a warrant the other day under the Lord chief Justices own hand, commanding us to work six days, and this old villain would persuade us to play twelve, he teaches also revelling and rebellion, we cannot bear any rule with our servants when he comes, for if we command them to follow their work, they will murmur and deny it, saying, Is it not *Christmas Time?*

Thus my Lord, and several other wayes, he is the author of Rebellion and sedition; in fine my Lord, he bring with him, bith fire, fuel, and bellows of contention. Thus being extream hasty about my labour, I desire your honour to excuse me.

Counc.

Go to industrius fool, labour for
    those,
Which ne're will thank thee; nay per-
    haps thy foes

Judg. Are there any more?
Clerk. Call Mr. *Mean-well.*
Cr. O yes, Mr. *Mean-well.*
Judg. Come fellow, what can you say?
Mean. My Lord, I can say that this Old man is a spend-thrift, a riotous spoyl-good, he is the chief cause that the good creatures are abused, he is a superstitious and an Idolatrous fellow, an ob-server of times, he makes his belly his god, a meer *Dives*, he fares deliciously every day, but his feasting is the cause of poor Lazarus his fasting.

He provokes only to wanton fulness, and lustful love, he makes those that love him & his company, unfit for any good duties; but on the contrary, he makes them ready for all evil, as uncleanness, scurrility, vain talking, and the like; he is like the Idolatrous *Israelites*, they ate and drank, no mention of grace before the meat, and rose up to play, there is no mention of grace after meat; just so doth he, he teaches that which the people of the old world practised, only eating and drinking &c such other delights: This was he, my Lord, that invited *Jobs* sons to dinner.

He overcomes men with surfeiting & drunkenness, and makes them that they cannot pronounce *Shiboleth;* he hath twelve sons, all follow the steps of their Father, and they keep company with one Mr. *Prodigal,* Mr. *Wastful, Belly-chear,* and *Idle,* with Mr. *Gamester,* and sucyh others like them, all the accursed brats of base men, here is a friend of mine, called Mrs. *Prudence,* she can inform your honour of something else.

Council.

> Thy name is *Mean-well,* friend, I
>   know 'tis so
> That thou art call'd, yet thou ne're
>   didst do.
> Thy Father he was call'd *Curious,* he
>   would know
> Whether the Rainbow had a string
>   or no,

What wood the man that's in the
   Moon doth carry,
   Or whether he intend or no to mary,
   Such Monsters, yea such Satyrs, and
   mad strains,
   Danc'd in the wilderness of his wild
   brains.

Cler. Call Mrs. *Prudence.*

Cr. O yes, Mrs. *Prudence.*

Judg. Make room for that Gentlewoman to come in. Come good woman, are not you a stranger hereabouts?

Prud. My Lord, wheresoever your honour is, I desire to be your hand-maid; as for my residence, it is most in the University, and here and there, sometimes in the Country, I am found as soon in a lowly cottage, as under a lofty Crown.

I have a sister called *Wisdome,* we always travel and dwell together.

Judg. Jury take a special notice of this womans testimony, and get as much acquaintance with her & her sister as you can. Come vertuous woman, let me hear what thou canst say in the behalf of the Common-wealth against the Prisoner.

Prud. My Lord, much hath been already spo-ken, and much more I can say, this Old man hath been one chief instrument that I and my daughters have been abused. I have three Daughters, my Lord, the first is called *Patience*, the second *Temperance*, the third *Chastity*, and one also named *Sobriety*, all these by this *Christmasses* means, are injuriously dealt withal, and violently handled, which before his coming, were in good estimation in Gentlemens houses; my Daughter *Patience* is an admirable good servant, she uses to look to the children and servants, and would keep them in love, peace, and quiet; if at any time she were reviled, she would not revile again.

Josephs words were often in her mouth, *See that ye fall not out by the way*; she is an excellent Labourer, and in the winter time of adversity, no Chiristian able to live without her, yet this naughty fellow, hath much wronged this my Daughter, and caused her to be thrown out of doors; for whersoever he is entertained, he carries a very base fellow called *Gamester* with him, and he hath two companions, the one called *Spendall*, and the other *Careless*; these will ride abroad night-times, vizarded, to glean money, to maintain their play, and make men stand, that would fain be going, and leave the stranger with a heavy heart, and light purse; This *Gamester* hath also one chief man called *Anger*, and also two Pages, the one called *Swearing*, the other *Cursing*, and when there is any difference about their Masters play, these two presently call in two others as good as themselves, one named *Quarrelling,* the other named *Fighting,* and these murder my Daughter *Patience.*

For my second Daughter *Temperance,* she is a very abstemious maid, and uses always to wait upon the Table, before his wicked wretch comes, and then she is banisht, or choaked, at the best thrown out of the doors; and then perhaps, must lye without in the street, no entertainment can get, if he be in this Town, unless it be at some honest Tradesmans house, it may be at the Ministers, if he be one of the last Edition.

My third Daughter *Chastity* is as beautiful as the Sun, and she is a Chamber-maid, and this fellow is the cause that she is abused also, for *Gluttony* hath two Associates, *Chambering & Wantonness,* & these kick my poor Daughters divers times down the stairs; Thus my Lord, my children, whom I have so educated, as they are fit companions for Prices, are my this vile Varlet abused; my Lord, in few words, he is the cause that many men make their Tables an Alter to their belly, and a snare to their souls.

Judg. Prudence, Many women have done vertuously, but thou hast excelled them all.

Pru. Good my Lord pity me.

Judg. I do, and will pity thee.

Coun.

> Good my Lord, your pity a while
> > withold,
> One Tale is good, until the other's
> > told.
> Hear but old *Christmas* what he says,
> > and then
> You will reserve some pity for
> > old men.

Judg. Old *Christmas* hold up thy head, and speak for thy self, thou hast heard thy inditement, and also what all these Witnesses have evidenced against thee, what sayest thou now for thy self, that sentence of condemnation should not be pronounced against thee?

Christm. Good my Lord, be favourable to an old man, I am above one thousand six hundred years old, and never was questioned at Sizes or Sessions before: my Lord, look on these white hairs, are they not a Crown of glory?

Judg. Yea, if they be found in a good way.

Christm. I hope you shall not find these in a bad way.

And first my Lord, I am wronged in being indited by a wrong name. I am corruptly called *Christmas*, my name is *Christ-tide,* or time.

And though I generally come at a set time, yet I am with him every day that knows how to use me.

My Lord, let the Records be searcht, & you shall find, that the Angels reejoyced at my coming, & sung *Gloria in excelsis;* the Patriarchs, and Prophets longed to see me.

The fathers have sweetly imbraced me, our modern Divines all comfortably cherisht me, O let me not be despised now I'm old. Is there not an injunction in *Magna charta,* that commands men to inquire for the old way, which is the good way, many good deeds do I do, O why do the people hate me? We are commanded to be given to Hospitality, & this hath been my practice from my youth upward: I come to put men in mind of their redemption, to have them love the other, to impart with something here below, that they have receive more & better things above; the wife man faith, *There is a time for all things,* & why not for thankfulness? I have been the cause, that at ny coming Ministers have instructed the people every day in the publick, telling the people how they should use me, & other delights, not to effeminate or corrupt the mind, & bid them abhor those pleasures from which they should not rife bettered, and that they should by no means turn pass-time into Trade: And if that at any time they have stept an inch into excess, to punish themselves for it,& be ever after the more careful to keep within compass.

And did also advise them to manage their sports without Passion, they would also tell me people, that their feasts should not be much more than nature requires; and grace moderates, not pinching, nor pampering: And whereas they say that I am the cause they sit down to meat, & rise up against graceless, they abundantly wrong me: I have told them, that before any one should put his hand in the dish, he should look up to the owner, & hate to put one morsel in his mouth unblessed: I tell them they ought to give thanks for that which is paid for already, knowing that neigher the meat nor the mouth, nor the man, are of his own making: I bid them fill their bellies, not their eyes, and rise from the board, not glutted, but only satisfied, and charge them to have a care, that their guts be no hindrances to their brains or hands, & that they should not lose themselves in their feasts, but bid them be soberly merry, and wisely free. I also advise them to get friendly Thrift to be their Caterer, and Temperance to carve at the board, and be very watchful that obscenity, detraction, and scurrility be banished the table, but let their discourse be as savoury as the meat, and so feed as though they did eat to live, not live to eat, and at last, rise as full of thankfulness, as of food: This hath, this is, & this shall be my continual practice. Now concerning the particulrs that these folks charge me with, I cannot answer them, because I do not remember them, my memory is but weak, as old mens use to be: but me thinks they seem to be the seed of the Dragon, they send forth of their mouths, whole floods of impious inventions against me, & lay to my charge things which I am not guilty of, which hath caused some of my friends to forsake me, and look upon me as a stranger: My brother *Good-works* broke his heart when he heard on it; my sister *Charity* was taken with the Num-palsie, so that she cannot stretch forth a hand: O tell it not in the City, nor publish it in the Country: my Lord, I am but a bad Orator, therefore I humbly desire your honour, to hearken to my Council and Witnesses.

> In the mean space, I'le weep, I
> cannot hold,
> Good works are dead, and charities
> half cold.

Judg. Councillor, what can you say?

Counc. Methinks my Lord, the very clouds blush, to see this old Gentleman thus egregiously abused; if at any time any have abused themselves by immoderate eating and drinking, or otherwise spoyl the creatures, it is none of this old mans fault, neither ought he to suffer for it: for example, the Sun and the Moon are by the heathens worshipt, are they therefore bad because idoliz'd, so if any abuse this old man, they are bad for abusing him, not he bad for being abused: These Bastard of *Amon,* have abused him, and therefore now would banish him: far be it from my Lord, to casheir a good thing, with the base use annexed thereunto: They term his charity wasting and spoiling, the making of Idlers, and incresing of Beggars: but where too much charity hath slain her thousands, too little hath slain her ten thousands: some of these witnesses did hint at Religion, but I believe they are Maidens for that, the first that woos them may win them: they tax him of Rebellion and sedition, but how can love and peace be the Author of that? For that is his Motto.

As for Mrs. *Patience,* because your honour is pleased to give more credence to her testimony, than to any of the rest, I shall answer her in particulars: and first for her children, I must confess, as she said, they are fit companions for Princes, but she slanders Old Father *Christmas,* to say that he ever wronged any of them; no, he ever had a good esteem of them, it was once *Anger,* a fiery Fellow, with *Wrath* and *Rage* his sons, that threw her

Daughter *Patience* out of doors, and not he: and for her Daughter *Temperance*, it was *Gouttony*, and unsatiable appetite, that abused her, and not this Old Man.

And for her Daughter *Chastity*, it was a scurvy scabby fellow, called *Carnal Concupiscence*, that forced her, therefore I beseech your honour give not any ear to these false reports. Then said the Judge, Mr. *Sheriff*, give order for the apprehending of these fellows, & presently after apprehending of them, execute them.

> Then drag them to the ditch, where
>   let them lye,
> So long as one man hath a memory.

Counc. My Lord, here are some honest men desire to give in their evidence in the old mans behalf.

Judg. Who are they, let them be called.

Clerk. Cryer, call *Simon Servant.*

Cr. O yes, *Simon Servant.*

Call *Peter Poor.*

Cr. Peter Poor.

Call *Nicholas Neighbourhood.*

Cr. Nich. Neighbourhood.

Judg. Come *Simon Servant*, what can you say in the behalf of the Old Man here?

Serv. My Lord, I live at the Town of *Bond*, in the County of little *Rest*; my Master is called Mr. *Hardheart*, a great enemy to this old father at the Bar; but for my own part, I will speak upon my oath, that I had suffered more than an *Egyptian* bondage, had it not been for him.

I had had a Sabbethless pursuit of my Masters labour, had it not been for him; the very beasts that groan under the burden are beholden to him for ease, for when the Ox and the Asses neck seemed married to the yoke, he diversed them; the very Jews had their Jubilees, times of rest; therefore, good my Lord, if you give us noting, keep not our brick and straw from us.

Judg. Peter Poor, what can you say?

Poor. My Lord, I dwell at the town of *Want*, in the County of *Needs*, poor in name and poor in estate; and had it not been for old *Christmas*, had had been poorer, if poorer I could have been: had it not been for him, my best friend *God-free Giving*, has lost his live; all that have spoken against him, are all *Gadarens*, and of the Linage of *Nabul* (Mrs. *Prudence* only excepted) if you take away this merry old Gentleman from us, you take away all our joy and comfort that we have on earth.

Hear us good Judge, we for thy
favour call,

Save him alive, or else destroy us all.

Clerk. Call Mr. *Neighbour-hood.*

Cr. O yes, Mr. *Neighbour-hood.*

Judg. Come friend, what can you say?

Neighbour. May it please you my Lord, I dwell at the Town of *Amity*, in the County of *Unity*, my Father was the good *Samaritan*, and my Mother was called *Dorcas*, and all that I can say for this Old Man is, that he is a very kind and loving man, inoffensive to all, a hater of strife, a lover of harmless mirth, our whole Town and County are much beholding to him when he comes, for he uses all means to bring us together, and to renew friendship; he is a great Peace-maker, if there have been any difference betwixt party and party, he will endeavour to end it in an amicable way: he always uses to tell me (next God) I must love my namesake, to glorifie the first, and tenderly affect the second: in fine, my Lord, he is as like Goodness as Charity can make him.

Moreover my Lord, he is our Land-mark, and it is forbidden in *Magna Charta* to remove the Land-mark.

Hica Busy. My Lord, there be four goodly persons more which have very material and convincing evidence against this old Delinquent at the Br, who crave admission.

26

Jud. What are their names and qualities?

Cler. Col. *Reynard*, a vagrant Brasier.

Judg. *A vagrant Brasier,* what's that?

Coun. *Crab.* A Tinker, my good Lord, certainly he is no enemy against *Christmas*, who hath so commonly browzed upon hospitality, and whose trade hath been to live upon the common decay of Kettles, Bowles, Bellows, & Brass pots, which are destroyed in the sweet service of *Christmas.*

Judg. *What are the other?*

Cler. Mr. *Truson* a Translator.

Jud. *A Translator of what?* Of Boots or Books?

Coun. Crab. A Cobler my Lord, a fellow meerly for his own ends, one that doth wax great by the destruction of souls, and would destroy *Christmas* at last.

Judg. *Proceed.*

Cler. Captain *Draw*, Brewer.

Coun. Doth he oppose us? Shall his Barrell head run a tilt against *Christmas?* Doth any man in the World grow rich upon more unnecessary excess than the Brewer? A man who cannot subsist upon sober draughts, but upon the reeling Riots of full bowls and high intemperance, moderate drinking would quite begger him.

Judg. *What is the other?*

Cler. Mr. *Tremble*, a Pin-maker by Profession, and a Quaker in Religion.

Coun. *Crab.* A man possest with a familiar spirit, who is a point of humility conceives no man above him, one that without all question, makes Nonsense his private study, for it is impossible he should deliver it so excellently ill without premeditation.

Judg. *Let them be all*, but orderly, admitted.

Cler. Cryer, call Col. *Reynard.*

Cr. O yes, Col. *Reynard* appear in Court here.

Judg. Come Col. *Reynard,* what have you to say against *Old Christmas*, the Prisoner at the bar?

Col. My Lord he is a Malignant, a high lover of Kings, Honour, & Nobility, a gret hater of Saints, Sectarists, and Souldiers; that which he calls Liberality, Bounty and Charity, may be of pernicious consequence to our new Commonwealth, in drawing a greater party of the people by the teeth, & raising a greater party of faction with his Reasons, then we shall be able to quell by our Religions; that which is a bright vertue in our friends, is a great evil in our enemies; & as an evil my not be committed that good may come of it, so in the contrary a good is dangerous, which introduceth an evil consequence: To conclude, therefore, if this Old Man may be permitted to carry on his high hospitality, we shall in small time have such a fat fed Army of *Chrismtas* Cormorants raised up against us, that although we have destroyed all the Arguments of the Father *Christmas*, we shall be all routed with Reasons of the Son. My Lord, look to it, and you Gentlemen of the Jury, it will be too late to consider, when his power is gotten above disputation; I would have his body lye in prison, and estate remain under sequestration.

> I am a Souldier, and we all agree,
> Prevention is the heart of policy.

Judg. *You have no more to say bu this then?*
Col. And I think enough my Lord.
Judg. *Proceed to the next.*
Cler. Cryer, call Mr. *Trueson.*

Cr. O yes, Mr. *Trueson* come in Court, and give evidence for the Common-wealth against the Prisoner at the Bar.

Judg. *What say you* Mr. *Truson? Speak out to the Jury.*

Mr. *Tru.* My Lord, although I am now underlaid with the title of Colonel, I have been a Translator, but I cannot find in any Translation, by express command, that we ought to observe the annual Festivity of *Christmas*, & the argument they bring that it hath been decreed by Councils, & continued by Authority Fof the Church, conduceth nor to my satisfaction, for I defie Churches, & will allow no Councils, but a Council of war, they were but men, who according to their temporary advantages by the power of their Churches raised these Festivals up, and we are men, who for our conveniences, by the strength of our Stables will pull them down, *Sic velo, sic jubeo.* [sic. Probably "sic volo, sic jubeo " -- "this I want, this I decree "]

    Judg. *You have said, proceed.*

    Cler. Cryer, call Col. *Dray.*

    Coun. Make room there for the *Dray.*

    Jud. *Col.* Dray, *What say you to the Prisoner?*

    Col. *Dray.* My Lord, If I should consider my particular interest before the common good, I have something to say for *Christmas,* he hath been always a good fellow, a friend to the Brewer, & so full of peace, that he would willingly have every Tub stand upon his own bottom: but when I perceived him facious, and that he stood up on defence of that *Goliah* Kingly Government, I though it necessary with my *David*-like courage to destroy him with my Slings, and have brought the land into such a moderate condition, that every man may be his own Prince, and his own Priest for his own profit, I will therefore furnish him with no more drink, for my Tubs shall be imployed in holier uses.

    Coun.

> The barrel is turn'd to a dub, a
> dub, dub
> And the Brewer hath told you a tale
> of a Tub.

Cler. Cryer, call Mr. *Tremble.*

Cr. Mr. *Tremble, Tremble,* make room for the Quaker: What doth he come in naked?

Trem. Thou must understand that the truth should be so: *What sayest thou to me?*

Cler. Speak to the Judge and Jury.

Judg. What can you say against Christmas, *in behalf of the State?*

Trem. Thou shalt know, that I acknowledge neither *Christmas,* nor the State, the one is Gluttony, the other Pride: *And what art thou?*

Cler. It is the Judge, Pull off your hat.

Trem. Here is even one Idol going to judge another: Oh, thou man of earth, *Judge not lest thou beest judged;* come down from thine high place, and humble thy self amongst thy brethren, until thou art as vile in thine own eyes as thou art in mine, for till

> The Spirit hath convinced thee of
> pride
> Thou art as great a sinner as *Christ-*
> *tide.*

Thy scarlet Gown, and the Harlot of *Babylons* Petticoat where both cut out of one piece.

Cry. *Tremble, you are too rude; Pull off your hat.*

Judg. *Let him alone, what dost thou say against* Christmas?

Trem. I speak to thee thou man of sin, that exaltest thy self above thy brethren: As for *Christmas,* he hath committed folly in *Israel,* and is already rewarded; he hath sold his birthright for a mess of Plumb-pottage: but thou art the very picture of Antichrist, therefore *Come down thou Lucifer.*

Judg. *Keep him back.*

Cler. Take him away, he doth disturb the Court.

Coun.

> The pinmaker in his own trade
> doth fail
> He makes a speech hath neither
> head nor tail.

My honoured Lord, here are three eminent persons, whose families are all ancient and honest, that humbly desire they may present their vindications in behold of the Old man.

Judge. *Their names.*

Cler. Sir *Peaceful Plenty* Kt. And Baronet. Sir *Charles Charity,* Kt. & Doct. *Holy-heart, a Divine.*

Judg. *Give them admitance.*

Cler. Call Sir *Peaceful Plenty.*

Cry. O yes, Sir *Peaceful Plenty* appear in Court; What can you say that judgment may not proceed against the prisoner?

Sir *Peac.* That is the judgment of all well-meaning men in Christendome, he should be freed, and with much reverence regarded: My Lord, do but consider the quality of his accusers, men that under pretense of being for the common good, have basely ingrossed the common plenty of this fruitful Nation, and hid it in obscure corners, who do avoid the celebration of *Christmas* for no other end but as they are sworn enemies to liberality: Persons that are known Gluttons in their own private families, but are featful that a publick Feast should betray them to public acts of bounty; who at a thanksgiving for the destruction of brothers bloud, engross whole Markets for their Gluttony, but in commemoration of him who shed his own blood to preserve ours, an unnecessary number of curious questions are started about the nicety of time, and whether it be by Apostolical injunction, therefore I beseech you, my Lord, and you Gentlemen of the Jury, let the quality of his accusers be considered.

When just *Job* was accus'd by false
    pretence,
We read the Devil gave in evidence.

Judg. Call *the next.*

Cler. Cryer, call Sir *Charles Charity.*

Cry. O yes, Sir *Charles Charity.* (if thou canst) accuse the prisoner at the Bar in behalf of the Common-wealth.

Sir *Ch.* I have more charity, and so should they have that have brought him hither.

Judg. *What can you say in defence of him?*

Sir *Ch.* This my Lord, that he hath done more good in twelve dayes, and twenty though Schismaticks have done in twelve years, he doth not only enjoy open hous-keeping, but open Church-keeping, where the soul is feasted with praying and preaching of Gods word, exhibition of Sacraments, and other prious Rites, pertinent and proper to the eternal Author of their devotion; his open heart hath relieved millions of distressed people, whilst the uncharitable hands of his persecutors have destroyed thousands, and fed upon the blood of their best benefactors.

That person is a most ungrateful
    liver,

Who begs the benefit, and kills the
Giver.

My Lord, I could say much more, which I sup-
pose will be more succinctly exprest in the brevity
of a reverand Doctor, who appears here upon the
same account.

Judg. *Call the Doctor.*

Cryer. Doctor *Holy-heart* appear in Court.

Judg. *Come Doctor, what say you?*

Doctor. With reverence to your honour, I am pro-
voked by my conscious to vindicate the clear integrity of this injured prisoner at the Bar, I have
observed all the trial, and do wonder what kind of
counterfeit creature abused your honour, by as-
suming the sacred person of Mrs. *Prudence,,* as if
Prudence, could be so blind not to distinguish betwixt the righteousness of *Christmas,* and the riots of
his Intruders, betwixt use and abuse, as if a Church
should be pulled down, because a pocket hath been
pickt in it; it is the newst kind of Prudence that ever
I read of. For *Christmas* I have thus much to say for
antiquity, he hath been well received by the best re-
formed Churches above nine hundred years, and
was highly reverenced in the primative purity
many hundreds years before Popery was hatched;
nor can this Festival be a suggestion of Antichrist

(as some object) for what advantge can it be to Antichrist that our Savious should have his birthday
celebrated; if our Accusers object we have no Scrip-
ture command for it, let them shew in what Scrip-
ture it is forbidden or let but equal Judges balance
the piety of Antiquity with our distract6ed times,
and then thence judge whether it is likely that we
should have more inspirtin or revelation in twenty
years, than the succession of many religious Ages in
nine hundred and sixty. For other Objections, I hold
them frivolous, and unfit for Answers.

After this speech the Jury were ordered by the
Judge to withdraw, and bring in their verdict, who
in very short time returned, and brought him in,
Not guilty, with their own judgement upon it.
That he who would not fully celebrate *Christmas,*
should forfeit his estate. The Judge being a man of
old integrity, was very well pleased, and *Christmas*
was released with a great deal of triumph and ex-
altation.

But as he walk'd they strewed all his
wayes
With Holly, Ivy, Rosemary and
Bayes.

The end of the Forenoon Tryal.

TO MR. ANTHONY SKINNER AND MR. JOHN BLOCK HIS BROTHER, MERCHANTS IN PLYMOUTH.

Gentlemen,

Just now is come into the harbour, the good Ship called the *Thankful Remembrance;* the Master of her is called *Old Christmas,* she is Laden with Hospitality, a Commodity that is very scarce; she could hardly escape Naufrage. The *Euroclydon* winds and waves conspired against her to dash her in pieces against the black rocks of Oblivion, where she had perished, had she not born up to the Cape of Good Hope. And although M. *Starve-mouse,* and Mr. *Cold-kitching* repine at his Landing, yet I know that both you wil congratulate the Master for his safe arrival;

And speedily to him resort,
And bid him welcome in your Port.

Yours,
J. K.

TO MY GOOD FRIEND MR. PHILIP PEARCE OF MODBURY.

Sir,

Here I present you with a New-no-thing for a New-years gift, I am ashamed of it, but I cannot now prevent it; I have been told that there have some been displeased with the former part, and I am sorry that I have offended my weak Brethren; let them forgive me this, and I will never trouble them with such a Toy any more.

And for your part you may me justly blame, Unto this worthless piece to set your name. But if there ought be here that like you do,

I pray fall to't, and much good do you too.

J. K.

THE AFTERNOON TRYALL OF CHRISTMAS.

To omit the various discourse which the Judges, Sheriffs, and Justices had a Dinner; when they were returned, and had taken their places on the Bench, they commanded to bring *Old Christmas* to the Bar; who when he came look't so smug and pleasant, his cherry cheeks appeared through his thin milk white locks, like lushing Roses vail'd with snow white Tiffany; or like the Lilly matcht with the Carnation, the true Emblem of Joy and Innocence; which the Judges having taken notice of, said, Methinks you put a good face upon't Old Man.

Chr.

An unstain'd Conscience of the Rack
can smile,

And makes a better face than wine
or oil.

Come, come said the Judges, are the Jury agreed? With that Sir *Hica* told the Judge, that one Mr. *Blind-zeal*, a man that had the greatest Estate in the Country, with Captain *Capons-face*, and Mrs. *All-tongue* his Sister did desire their Evidence might be taken in the behalf of the Common-wealth; and also requested the Judge; that such as were well-affected as they, might have the benefit of a Council as their Antagonist had.

Judg. I will give all liberty and freedom for a Legal proceeding, and will take all pains that may be to give all parties, if possible, satisfaction; and to tis purpose Sir *Hica* chuse your Counsellor, and let the witnesses be call'd on both parts that have not yet appeared: And you Jury, give your best attention, for it concerns the life of the Old man.

With that Sir *Hica* busie, delivered a Fee to one Counsellour *Verjuce*, a sowre look't fellow; but Counsellour *Crab* seemed not dismaid at his Pig-looks, but looked Pig-again: in the mean time there stood up a Country fellow, and called to the Judge and said, My Lord, if your Honour be at Put, it is stop game, for there be two Knaves a-board; meaning the two Counsellors: to whom the Judge replyed;

Jud. Sirrah, sirrah, be silent, or you shall be put, where you shall neither see light, nor Sun this sennight.

Country fell. Then goodnight Sir.

Then there was a List delivered to the Clerke, of those that had not yet appeared against the Old man in the forenoon; then the Judge commanded they should be called.

Cler. Cryer, Call Mr. *Blind-zeal.*

Cry. O yes, Mr. *Blind-zeal.*

Coun. Crab.

> Zeal it is blind, if knowledge doth
> not guide;
> Knowledge is lame, if not by zeal
> supply'd.

Judg. Where is the Witness that was call'd? Cannot he find the way in? Is there never a Scholar to help lead him?

Crab.

> No, as for such, he wish them
> hang'd and dead;
> The furious fool, will not be taught
> nor led.
> To rost an Egg he as much fire doth
> make,

As judgment for to roast an Ox doth
    take.

Judg. Come friend, what can you say?

Blinz. My Lord, this Old wretch *Christmas* at the Bar, I hate him with an inveterate hatred, he hath been an utter undoer of many a good friend of mine; my Lord it's great pity that the Cockatrice had not been crusht in the shell, then had the life of many a Creature been saved, for he hath been a Murtherer from the beginning; at his coming scarce an house in the Countrey, but there is one or other dead in it; he hath a younger brother called Mr. *Lent,* he hath always hated his bloudy practises, and openly by Proclamation hath detested them, and Enacted penalties by a Law to be levied on those that follow any of his rioutous courses; yet this milde Gentlemen, Mr. *Lent,* hath been long sick, and we fear he will hardly recover; but if he do die, I will swear this Old man hath been the death of him. Therefore, my good Lord, let Justice be executed upon him as a Murtherer.

Coun. Crab.

Away blind fool, do'st thou not life
    regard,
To hang him first, and judge him af-
    terward?

Coun. Verj. I would have you know *Crab* that this Gentlemen that last exprest himself, is as virtuous and Religious as you are profane and base, and were it not in this honourable presence, I could kick you below scorn, as once I raised you above your expectation.

Coun. Crab. You Vinegar face. Your mothers bottle, and the Ink-mans barrell were Couzen germans.

Coun. Verj. Sirrah do not quarrel.

Jud. What Witnesses are there more?

Cler. Cryer, call Captain *Capons-face.*

Cry. O yes, Captain *Capons-face.*

Jud. Captain, what can you say in the behalf of the Common-wealth against the Prisoner at the bar?

Coun. Crab. I'le cut his coxcomb by and by.

Capt Capons-face. My Lord I was told that in the forenoon he stood upon his justification, and denied that ever he was the Author of Sedition. Now, my Lord, I can prove that at the Town of *Stomach,* in the County of *Corps,* he hath been the chief cause of Mutiny and Insurection; for when Captain *Hot,* and Lieutenant *Cold,* Collonel *Roast,* and Major *Boild,* Ensign *Fish* and Serjeant *Fowle,* and Corporal *Flesh,* with other Common Souldiers meet [text blanked] the guard, there must needs be a [text blanked]to the great detriment of the C [text blanked] wealth of Nature. And furthermore, my Lord he causeth men to dig their own graves with their Teeth: He makes the Drunkard sing whilst the drink is sighing. And thus in short is that I can say.

Coun. Crab. This was that Bountiful Gentlema, my Lord, that promised his Souldiers, that whosoever did kill the Lion, he would give him the skin for his Labour; I never heard that ever he was so forward as any of his Company, except once at a Rout, and then he out-ran them all.

> And I commend his men, 'twas
>   wisely done,
> To give their Captain the first place
>   to run.
> And when his Worship pleased to
>   run away,
> 'Tis breach of Discipline for them to
>   stay.
> And he unto that Market seldom
>   goes,
> Where there is nothing to be sold
>   but blows:
> And when he to his over-match doth
>   came,
> He hath his handful, yet goes empty
>   home.

Coun. Verj. You are a base reviling *Rabsheka* Rascal, it is not thy black-mouthed Envy, nor Toad-coloured Malice, shall any way obscure the splendour and renown of this Captains fame.

Jud. Silence, I will have no more of this: What other Witnesses are there?

Cler. Cryer, call Mrs. *All-tongue.*

Cr. O yes, Mrs. *All-tongue.*

Jud. Come woman, where dwell you?

All-tongue. My Lortd, I dwell at the Town of *Tattle* in the County of *Prate*, my Maiden name is *All tongue*, but I have since been married to one *Mark Makebate*, by whom I had two Daughters, the one called *Tel-tale*, the other *Back-bite*; my Daughter *Back-bite* is but a sneaking wenmch; but my Daughter *Tel-tale* is a bold wench, she hath indeed committed a fault, she hath had a Bastard by an old Rogue, the brat is called *Lying*, yet neverthelesse, she is much made of at every house she comes at, and brings away with her in her lap abundance of Belly Timbr: And her chief practice is, to get the Mistress or Maids into a corner, and there she sweetly drops her rare inventions into the dripping pans of their ears, and her conclusion is always this, Be sure you do not tell who told you.

Jud. Woman, surely thou art not unfitly named:

this is nothing to the purpose, What canst thou say against the Old man at the Bar?

All-tongue: My Lord, When first I began to see the vanity of all humane Ordinances, I took especiall notice of the notirious and vile miscarriages of this Pharisaicall *Old Christmas*, who strives to colour all his beastiality with the paint of *Charity*. Me thought I loved him when he was a youth, he was a pretty plum pleasant boy; but his friends (as Parents use to do) doted too much on him, and that spoil'd him. They put him to a Tutor called Mr. *Sense,* one of the Fellows of the College of *Pleasure*, and all the Lectures ever he read to him were *Epicurean*, he brought him up only to sing and Play, Dance, Carrose and Complement, One time my Lord, I came along with the Carrier (and indeed I am seldome out of his company) and standing under this *Christmasses* Chamber window to hearken, as I commonly do at every bodies house, there I heard him playing and singing this profane Song to his Instrument:

SONG

> *Let us eat, drink and play;*
> And freely injoy,
> Whatsoever our natures desire;
> Whil'st we live on the Earth.
> Let our hearts stew in Mirth,
> Sweetly, over Concupiscense fire.

By this you may perceive, what a precious blade he is, my Lord.

Nay one thing more, may it please your Honour, I had almost forgotten, that he comes ten dayes into the *Netherlands* before he comes hither, and in the time of the Wars, there he drank healths with the Drunken *Dutchmen,* to the confusion of the *English*; My Lord, let your pity and compassion, banish him out of our Nation.

Coun. Crab. Sir, I tell your Honour what this Woman is, one Mr. *Earle,* that was well acquainted with her, gave me a Character of her, in which he told me that she did think her Purity consisted much in clean linnen: And that because she hath heard the Rag of *Rome,* she thinks it a very sluttish Religion, and rails at the Whore of *Babylon* for a very naughty woman; she left her Virginity as a Relique of Popery: she has no room for Charity, and understands no good works, but what are wrought on the Sampler; nothing angers her so much, as that Woman cannot preach: but what she cannot do at church she does at the Table, till a Capons sing silence her.

> But now I'le cease, lest I your pa-
> tience wrong.
> Or thought to be a Kins-man to All-
> tongue.

Coun. Verj. Your Sirrah, *Crab,* I knew when you were but a Hedger; my Lord, there is no credit to be given to what he hath spoken, for he will lie as cheap as a beggar, and as loud as a Clock.

Jud. Christmas, Canst thou say nothing for thy self? Thou hast heard what hath been Evidenced against thee.

Christmas. My Lord, their Allegations are to

vain, I conceive them not worth answering: but only to Mrs. *All-tongues* accusation for being in the *Netherlands*. My Lord, if plain truth may be believed, I shall need no Atturney in that cause; it was my hap to come thither when the Councel was held at *Dort,* where the most learned and Eminent Divines in Christendome were assembled, amongst t'whom I was courteously entertained, joyfully received and piously approved, which they conspicuously demonstrated, and by their charity to the poor manifested; and by divers other General Councels, I have been lovingly embraced, and of the necessity of my observation, they have testified, as that of

Generall Councells approving *Christmas.*

Nice.
Armenia.
Antioch.
Carthage.
Chalcedon.
Orleance.
Constantinople.
Ferraria.
Constance.
Basil.

Captain Capons-face. My Lord, This was he that

in the forenoon complained of his memory; I warrant your Honour, if he were searcht, we should
find a worse Diary about him, than was found in
B *Lauds* pocket.

Judg. Search him then.

Counf. Crab. Go Pick-pockets, doe, doe.

With that the Captain runs to him, and pulls
out a paper, and cryes out, Here 'tis, here 'tis.

Judg. Give it to the Clerk to read.

The Clerk having received it, read it out audi-
bly. The contents were these;

> Good people if I live or die,
> Be sure you follow Charity;
> For its power it is no lesse,
> Than to make Heaven to Earth
>   depresse.
> And again, it earth can make
> A flight above the Star's to take.
> 'Twas that made immortalitie,
> To become mortal, and t'di.
> Charity, is that which say,
> Come ye blessed, come away.
> Its power is such, that it can make
> The dumb to speak, the dead to
>   wake.

And whether I do live or die,
Be sure remember Charity.

With that there was a great shout, and many came in running with distracted looks, and told the Judge that all the Town was up in Arms, to come rescue the Old man; and before they made an end of speaking, in came half a dozen resolved Blades, and delivered a paper to the Judge, in which was this written;

We who unto this paper doe
    subscribe,
Not mov'd by Faction, nor expect no
    bribe.
But do unto your Lordship thus
    declare,
That the Old man that now is at
    the Bar;
Unless he be with honour quickly
    freed,
We tell you what you must expect
    with speed.
Those that endeavour Christmas to
    undo,
Will quickly down with Law and
    Judges too.

Hereupon Sir *Leonard Love-Peace*, the High-Sheriff, was ordered to take care for the Security of the Court, and the Prisoner, to suppress Routs, Riots and Tumults, and if he thought necessary to raise the Power of the County for that purpose.

Mr. *Sheriff.* My Lord, I have already taken necessary care for the Prevention and Supression of such Disorders; These were only a few unruly Apprentices, that came to shew their good-will to the Prisoner, because he was ever a Friend to them, and us'd to replenish the Exchequor of their Box; a remedy which they must certainly lose, if the Old-man mis-carry.

Coun. Verj. My Lord, here are two more substantial witnesses we desire may be heard against the Prisoner, the learned Sir *Musty Make-bate*, and the worshipful Squire *Flant of Mock-beggars Hall.*

Cry. Sir *Musty Make-bake*, and Squire *Flant* come into the Court, make room there, I think in my Conscience the Door is too little for the Squire's new Pantaloons.

Judg. Well, Sir *Musty*, what can you say against the Prisoner?

Sir Musty. My Lord, I have been a great Reader in my time, and have searcht narrowly into the Prisoners Pedigree, and find that he is a meer Counterfeit; for my Lord whereas he pretends the 25th of *December* to be his Day, the true *Christmas* happened a great deal sooner, even about the latter end of *September*, or beginning of *October*, as I have several Books affirm; and ought then to be observed; therefore I cannot but disown this Pretender, and conceive he deserves to suffer the Justice of the Court, for thus boldly personating another.

Coun. Crab.

> A shrewd Objection 'tis, but hold
>   Beloved,
> 'Tis roundly said, but not so squarely
>   proved;
> This Man reads Books, and loves it
>   as his life,
> If ought he meet with many en-
>   courage strive.

Judg. Come Squire *Flant*, what have you to say?

Flant. My Lord, I say this *Christmas* is a pitiful mechanick, gutling Fellow, Company for none but Plow-men, and Carters, and regarded only by a few Yeoman of *Kent,* or here and there an out-of-fashion'd Gentleman, that loves to walk in the dull ways of his Fore-fathers, and live at the same rate his great Grandsires did, in the days of Queen *Dick*; whereas the true bred Gallant and man of

Quality, in this our refined Age, manages his Affairs at another strain. He has something else to do with his money, than to keep open house for pampering the Paunches of a parcel of lubberly Clowns, and have the Pavement of his Hall spoiled with the dancing of their Hobnails; and therefore when this troublesom Fellow comes abroad cannot endure the Country for him, but as soon as ever *Michaelmas* Rent is received, to avoid his Impertinences, flips up to *London* in a Stage-Coach, and there lodges privately till his Jury of Cormorants, call'd the Twelve Days, are past, to save charges.

Coun. Crab.

    Rare Husbandry indeed: What
        heretofore
    Was spent on Tenant, and the Neigh-
        bouring Poor,
    Is now consum'd in private on a
        whore.

My Lord, The prosecutors have now gone through their whole Evidence, your Lordship has heard them with patience; Their Allegations are so weak, frivolous and impertinent, that I shall not abuse your Lordship's time by going about to refute them, but submit the Innocense of my Clients

Cause wholly to the Integrity of the Jury, and your Lordships Justice.

Whereupon the Jury without stirring from the Bar, affirmed their former Verdict and pronounced Old Father *Christmas* in wise guilty of the Indictment he stood charged with.

Which Verdict streight was wel-
com'd with the loud
Shouts and Applauses of the joyful
Crow.

Then the Judge arose and delivered his final determination.

*The Judges Sentence and Directions to Father
Christmas.*

You, the Prisoner at the Bar; since upon a fair Tryal you have been acquitted by your Country, I do here publickly declare you Innocent, and set you free from your Confinement. But for avoiding all such Scandals as here have been cast upon you, for the future, do not think fit to admonish you; that you remember your Office is not so much to feast the Body, as to refresh the Soul, by thankful and pious Meditations, on that wonderful Art of Divine Love, in the Sacred Incarnation which you annually commemorate: And that therefore as you are to promote mutual Love and Hospitality amongst Neighbours, and Charity to the Poor, so you are strictly to avoid and banish all Gluttony, Drunkenness, Wantonness and Prophaness; lest you turn the Festival of the Holy Jesus into a Sacrifice to *Bacchus*; and instead of keeping his Day, dishonour and crucifie the Lord afresh by whole name you are called. And lastly, that as you use Sobriety, so likewise use Prudence in your Entertainments, every one according to his Quality and Abilities,

> For though on Christmas something
>   may be spend,
> Yet not to make the whole year after
>   Lent.
> Observing these directions you will
>   recover,
> Your Ancient dignity and Primitive
>   Honour.

And put to silence the Fanatical Clamors of such ignorant Zealots, and foolish men, as have this day shown themselves your Adversaries.

The jolly Old Father Bow'd his Reverent Head very respectfully to the Court, thanking them not so much for his Acquital (for in that they did but serve their own Justice) as for this wholsom advice, which he declared himself resolv'd henceforth religiously to observe. And so the Court broke up.

And Christmas streight was courted
far and near,
To each good house to taste their
plenteous chear.

FINIS.